The World of Farm Animals

Ton van Eerbeek

BALLOON BOOKS™

What are dairy products?

* Foods that are made from milk.

COW

Cows produce milk.
Farmers have milk machines
that pull the milk from their udders.

A cow makes milk
only when it has given birth
to a calf. The milk is actually intended
for feeding the calf. A male calf is called a bull calf.

Did you know that cows have four stomachs?

3

What is a male goat called?

* A billy goat.

GOAT

This is a nanny goat. The farmer milks her twice a day. Goat cheese is made from the milk. Goats eat grass, twigs, and leaves.

In early spring, most nanny goats give birth to two babies. As the babies grow older, they like to jump and climb.

Did you know that young pygmy goats are no larger than a cat?

HORSE

What are horseshoes used for?

* To protect horses' hooves.

Horses were once used to pull farm equipment. Nowadays, they are used for recreation.

Baby horses are
called foals. Foals are usually
born in the spring. Foals are able
to run a few hours after they are born!

What is a mane?
* The hair on a horse's neck.

Why do pigs roll in the mud?

* To cool themselves.

PIG

Female pigs are called sows. They usually give birth to 10-15 piglets each year.

The piglets must not
get cold, so farmers place them
under a lamp to keep them warm. After
six months, they can weigh as much as 200 pounds!

9

Where are the largest sheep herds found?

* In Australia.

SHEEP

Sheep are raised for their wool. Before summer, they are sheared. Wool is made from their fleece.

A female sheep is called an ewe. In spring, females usually give birth to two lambs. Lambs are immediately able to stand upright once they are born.

What is a male sheep called?

*A ram.

DONKEY

How long does a donkey live?

* About 30 years.

The donkey belongs to the horse family. Donkeys are calm, strong animals that like to eat hay and grass.

They enjoy company and attention. They are very curious and are certainly not dumb! They make a sound called a bray. It can be heard from far away.

What do you call a cross between a horse and a donkey?

*A mule.

How long have people had dogs as pets?

* More than 12,000 years.

DOG

Every farm has a watchdog or a herding dog. There are more than 100 different dog breeds.

A Collie is in this
picture. Puppies are born
blind and deaf. After three or four
weeks, they begin to hear and to walk around.

How long does a dog live?

* 10-15 years, sometimes longer.

CAT

How long does a cat live?

* 13-17 years.

There are always a few cats around a farm. They catch mice that live in the stables and in the hay.

Young cats are called kittens. Their eyes are closed at birth. All kittens have blue eyes. Later, their eyes turn a different color.

What do you call the sound a happy cat makes?

* Purring.

What does "Don't count your chickens before they hatch!" mean?

* To take things one step at a time.

CHICKEN

A chicken is a bird, but it almost never flies. Most farmers have a few hens and one rooster.

18

Hens lay eggs. A brooding hen keeps her eggs warm for about three weeks before the chicks hatch. They are covered with down. Later, they grow feathers.

*A chicken that may run free.

What is a free-range chicken?

Did you know that a goose lives to be 30 years old?

GOOSE

Geese are large, heavy birds. They are good swimmers, but they search for grass to eat on land.

The male goose
watches over the female
while her eggs hatch. If anyone comes
too close, he will gaggle and blow loudly.

* Soft pillows and comforters.

What is made from goose feathers?

Did you know that duck chicks swim right away?

DUCK

Ducks are waterfowl.
They search for insects and plants
in the water. Duck eggs are larger than chicken eggs.

A duck
broods for about
five weeks. The hatched chicks
immediately follow their mother.

What is a collective name for ducks, geese, and chicken?

* Poultry.

Index

Billy goat, 4

Boar, 9

Calf, 3

Cat, 16, 17

Chick, 19

Chicken, 18, 19

Collie, 15

Cow, 2, 3

Dog, 14, 15

Donkey, 12, 13

Duck, 22, 23

Ewe, 11

Foal, 7

Goat, 4, 5

Goose, 20, 21

Hen, 18

Horse, 6, 7

Kitten, 17

Lamb, 11

Mule, 13

Pig, 8, 9

Piglet, 9

Puppy, 15

Pygmy goat, 5

Ram, 11

Rooster, 18

Sheep, 10, 11

Sow, 8

Source of the illustrations:
Photographs by HR Tierfoto and Diapress